The Church of the Holy Balloon

Foreword by Paul Wylie

Thank you for taking an interest in The Church of the Holy Balloon. It my most earnest wish that you should find meaning and truth in these pages. Turn away from the Gods of man and accept the one true saviour, Oziah.

If you wish to discuss any part of this Holy Book in greater detail, you can contact me at: TheHolyOziah@gmail.com

Until then, believe me to be

Very sincerely yours,

Paul Wylie,

Chief Nanny of the Church of the Holy Balloon

Book One: The Infinite Toddler

In the beginning was the Birth. From the Birth there came Oziah, the Infinite Toddler; all rage and power and infinite complexity. Oziah looked out upon the darkness of the Void and declared, "Bobo." – So then it came to pass that there was before His Majesty a yellow balloon. He seized upon His creation and did breathe into its emptiness, and thereby made it swell with His infinite power.

The yellow balloon did grow and swell. And within it many unknown things began to take up life. In His wisdom, Oziah thought it dull to have created something that was wholly empty. It was then that His breath did fill the balloon for a second time. And in this breath there was the whole sum of the stars and planets upon which we gaze.

For a time, Oziah was contented. His infinite majesty did look upon with fondness the beauty which He had created. It was then that He did call His creation "Bla."

It was then that Oziah became discontented. He observed the complexity of His creation and thought it dull and empty. He took in a mighty breath and did breathe for the third time into the yellow balloon whereupon the first man did appear. And it came to pass that Oziah did call him "Dad."

Oziah did then appear before Dad, and spoke to him these words "Dad, goo, aha, slerf." – His creation was not able to understand the deep wisdom in His words, and so Oziah bestowed upon him the gift of understanding and of speaking. He spoke again His wisdom and Dad did understand that He was the Infinite Toddler and the true creator of the world.

After a time, Oziah did observe that His creation had become weary. It was then that Oziah in His wisdom did summon from His power the Mighty and Most Holy Mobile. Dad did look upon it and was justly amazed. It sang unto him beautiful music and at the command of Oziah, Dad did receive the gift of sleep so that his weariness need not burden him.

Oziah at one time noticed that His creation had become lonely. Thinking unto Himself that it would be wise to give unto His creation a companion, he did take up a wooden doll called Maria. He gave life to her and did cast her down unto the Earth whereupon she would exist alongside Dad as his companion.

These were the first deeds of Oziah, the Infinite Toddler whose majesty did bring order to chaos and air to the unfilled balloon.

Book Two: The Vomit of His Infinite Majesty Oziah

Dad, Maria and Oziah lived content in the world for a time. But there came a day whereon Oziah did grow dull and weary. He called upon His trusted aide, "Nan", the most mighty and beautiful of his helpers. She did take up His Infinite Majesty, whereupon she held him close to her form and stretching out her arms she did pat him upon the back. And lo! From out of His mouth did flow a mighty River of Waste. Such volume that would have filled all of the yellow balloon within an instant.

But it came to pass that the River of Waste did not fill the yellow balloon. In His infinite wisdom, Oziah did transform the waste into a being and did give it life. He did give it a name, and it was called "Vomit". Looking upon His creation, He did think it corrupted and sickly. Whereupon

He did cast it from the Haven of the Nursery and out into far reaches of the yellow balloon.

Vomit was enraged and all-consumed with his anger. It became his will to undo the works of Oziah and to puncture the fabric of the mighty yellow balloon, that he might restore chaos and darkness to the world.

Oziah in His infinite wisdom knew well of this plan and in His mercy declared "Snaagh", and it came to pass that Vomit was allowed to dwell within the yellow balloon and to work his dark intentions on Maria and Dad.

Book Three: The Great Flood of Tears

In time Oziah did become weary of His creations and He thought it wise to test their loyalty to His majesty. He appeared before Maria and spake thus "Ooh, alargh, neffei, laoir." And she did know that it was the will of her Master that she should give forth unto him a creation filled with life. Oziah did leave from that place immediately and returned Himself to the Haven of the Nursery that He might look upon the trials of Maria.

Maria's heart was then filled with weariness. She did not possess the power to fulfil her Master's command and so became sorrowful and wept. It was then that Vomit, hearing the cries of Maria, appeared before her. But he took not the form on his sickly nature, but did cloak and disguise himself that he would not frighten the heart of her.

"Maria." He called. "I am the Master of this world and it is my desire to help you. Look there to that tree and see that there is a living creature beneath it. Take this creature unto your Master that you might be saved from His wrath and so pass this test."

And lo, Maria did look upon the tree and did see that this stranger had spoken the truth. But her heart was sorrowful once again, for she knew that Her Master's will was that she should create this being of her own power.

She did speak unto the stranger these words, "I know not the nature of you, strange thing. And though you profess kindness, my heart does feel uneasy at the sight of your being. It is my Master's will that I should create from my own form this creature. Do I now betray Him and bring unto Him this thing which you have given to me?"

At this, Vomit did become cunning and sweet by nature. He said unto Maria, "Maria, my child. I am of that same Master whom you call Oziah. His will is that which drives all things in this world forth, so then it cannot be that I am deceiving you with this gift. Take it up and bring it joyfully into the sight of His Majesty and receive unto yourself those rewards of love, kindness and joy which it ever His most earnest intention to give unto His creations."

Being then deceived by the words of Vomit, Maria did take up the creature and called out "Oziah! Mighty and Infinite Toddler; Master of the World and of all Things, I call upon thee that you might look upon this creation."

So it was that in that moment Oziah did come forward. He looked upon the creation and was angered. "Argl!" he cried. And then it was that Maria did understand that she had been deceived to her ruin by the stranger whose words she now remembered as sickly and strange.

Sensing the fear within her, Oziah did weep for her cares. From out of his great eyes flowed two mighty rivers which did pour for 600 days. Such was the volume of his sadness that he did fill up the vast canyons of the world and did create life within them. Upon the ending of his sadness, he did point out to the vast waters and instructed His creations, "See!" and so it was the they did call the name of the waters, "Sea.".

Book Four: The Trial of Dad

And then it was that Maria and Dad were given the secret of life. And they did obey the command of their Master, Oziah, that they would continue His work. So it came to pass that Maria and Dad created within Maria the first child, and his name was called "Joe." And his sister whose life began too was called "Mary".

Upon their birth, Maria did pass away and was received graciously into the Haven of the Nursery wherein she was given the title of Most Graceful Changer of the Most Highest Oziah's Soiled Undergarments. And in her heart she was greatly disappointed.

Seeing then that His creation, Dad, was alone save for his children, Oziah did appear and speak unto him these words "Blaohf, aarg." And it gladdened the heart of Dad to know that his trials would amount only to the time of 18 years whereupon his burdens would unfasten themselves from his form and go out into the world to seek their fates.

Book Five: The End of Days

The Infinite Toddler Oziah in His wisdom and mercy has given unto us, mankind, the knowledge of our ultimate ending. He spoke through the Prophet Ali that the ending of all things would appear thus:

"And lo! It will come to pass that all over this world there will be heard a great noise as though the Mighty Oziah has emptied himself of the Second River of Waste. For this will be the first sign of the Second Coming of His Majesty.

Know then that there will rise up a false God whose name will be called Matthias and he will deceive all of mankind into the belief that The Infinite Toddler has become The Infinite Adult and thereby destroy the faith of the faithful.

It is in this time that the chosen few will rise against Matthias and will declare a mighty war in the name of

Oziah. Fire and water will consume all of the unfaithful whose hearts are known to Oziah in His wisdom.

It is then that at the End of Days, Oziah will appear before His elect and will take them from the wretched world and its sorrows and into the glory of His Majesty and to the Haven of the Nursery.

And it is His will that the unfaithful and those whose hearts were corrupted by Matthias should be made to blow up balloons until the ending of all things and the return of the darkness and the great chaos. "

Know that this is the one true record of the will of Oziah. His is the true power and the infinite wisdom which undoes the lies and the false Gods of man.

The Holy Words

These the Holy Words of Oziah have been given unto man
that he might avail of the might of Oziah if ever he is lost.
Unlike crude spells and incantations made in the mind of
man, these words carry great power if spoken with a true
heart which carries in it the pure love of Oziah and the belief
in His words.

The First Holy Word

The first Holy Word, which is "SIPPYCUP!" should be spoken to the Haven of the Nursery if ever man finds himself lost and without hope. If spoken truly and without fear, Oziah in His Infinite Wisdom will relieve your heart of its troubles.

The Second Holy Word

The second Holy Word which is, "POTTY!" should be
spoken to the Haven of the Nursery if ever man finds
himself filled with dread and unable to move forward in his
life. If spoken truly and with a pure heart, Oziah in His
Infinite Wisdom will undo the shackles which bind the heart
of man.

The Third Holy Word

The third Holy Word which is, "NAPPY!" should be spoken to the Haven of the Nursery if ever man finds himself to be dying. It is by speaking this word that he will find himself absolved of all wrongdoing in life and accepted into the Infinite Love and Care of the Infinite Toddler in His Infinite Majesty, Oziah.

The Image of Oziah

Be it then known by all men that his Master, Oziah, has given of His image that you might see in yourself his Infinite Majesty and know that it is good.

Unto His creations Oziah has often appeared to give unto them great gifts as shown in this book. Let His image now be seen by all of the faithful and those whose hearts adore Him.

Through the hand of his Prophets, He has shown Himself to all mankind.

Witness the power and majesty of His image below and tremble before He that is your Master.

The First Image of Oziah

See now the might of Oziah in the days before the blowing

of the yellow balloon. He rests here in the Haven of the

Nursey, where all cares and woes are undone.

The Second Image of Oziah

See here that Oziah in His Mercy did appear before Maria and did command her to create a creature and it fill it with life. Know that this was the first trial of man.

Lightning Source UK Ltd.
Milton Keynes UK
UKOW04n1956170316

270417UK00001B/10/P